MANDALAS
COLORING BOOK

4 BOOKS IN 1!

DELUXE EDITION

DOVER PUBLICATIONS, INC.
MINEOLA, NEW YORK

NOTE

Taking its name from the Sanskrit word for "circle," the mandala is a Hindu and Buddhist symbol that represents the universe and its energy. Traditionally used for meditation, the repetitive patterns draw the eye to the center of the circle to provide a pleasing focal point. Here you'll find over 100 finely detailed mandala designs perfect for the experienced colorist. Plus, perforated pages make it easy to display your work.

Bibliographical Note

Mandalas Coloring Book: Deluxe Edition is a new compilation of previously published Dover books by Marty Noble, Randall McVey, and Alberta Hutchinson. See source information below.

Source Information

Mystical Mandala Coloring Book (2007), *Mesmerizing Mandalas* (2012), *Nature Mandalas* (2012), *Square Mandalas* (2012).

International Standard Book Number

ISBN-13: 978-0-486-77931-7
ISBN-10: 0-486-77931-9

Manufactured in the United States by Courier Corporation
77931904   2014
www.doverpublications.com

NATURE
MANDALAS

MARTY NOBLE

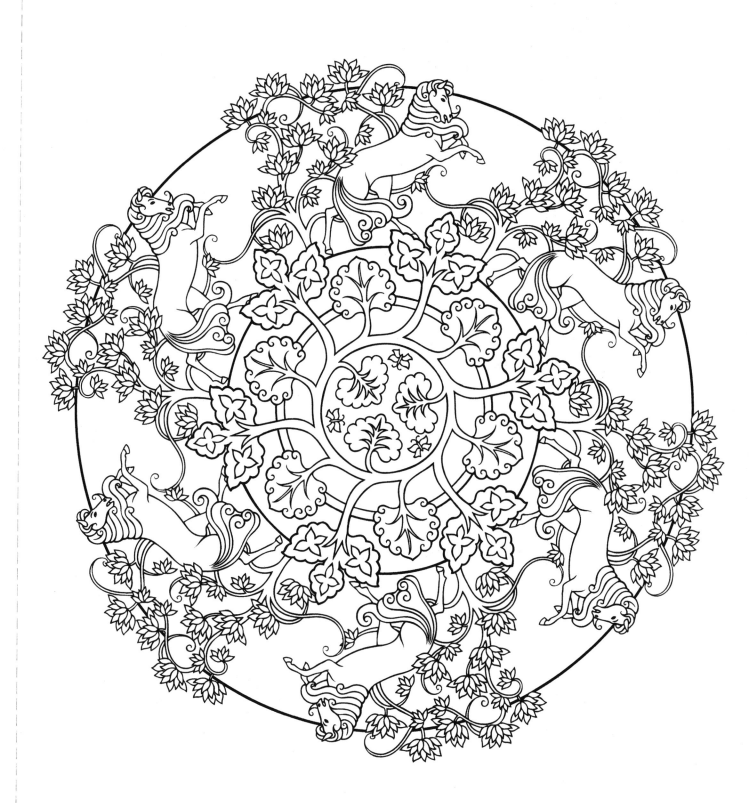

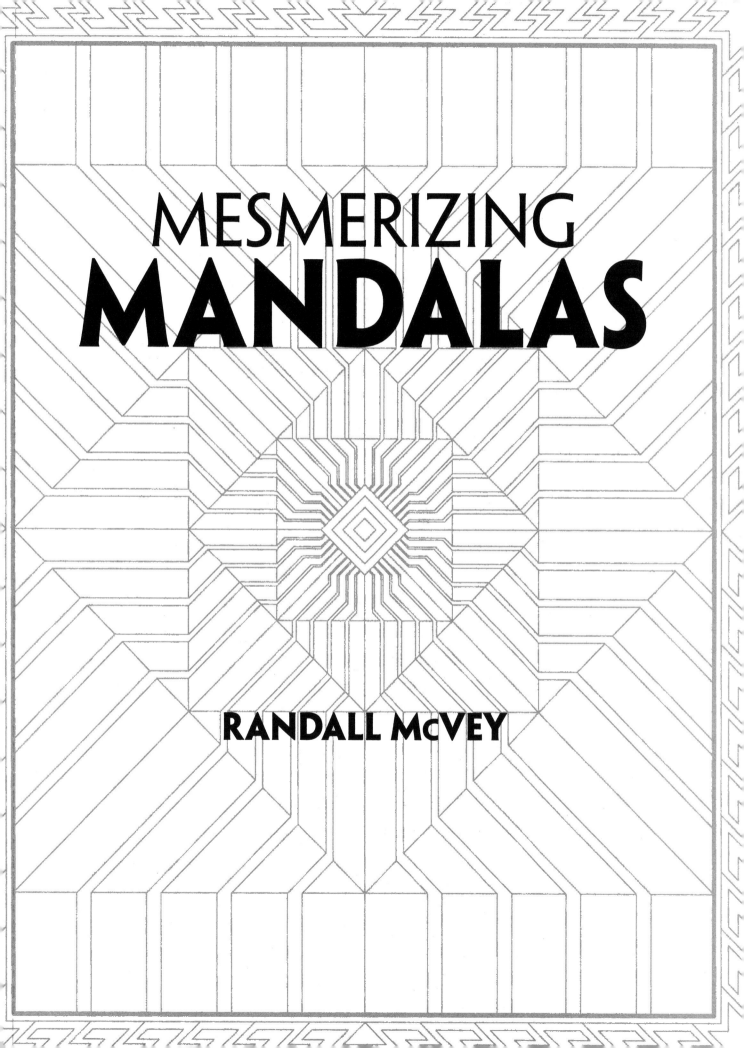

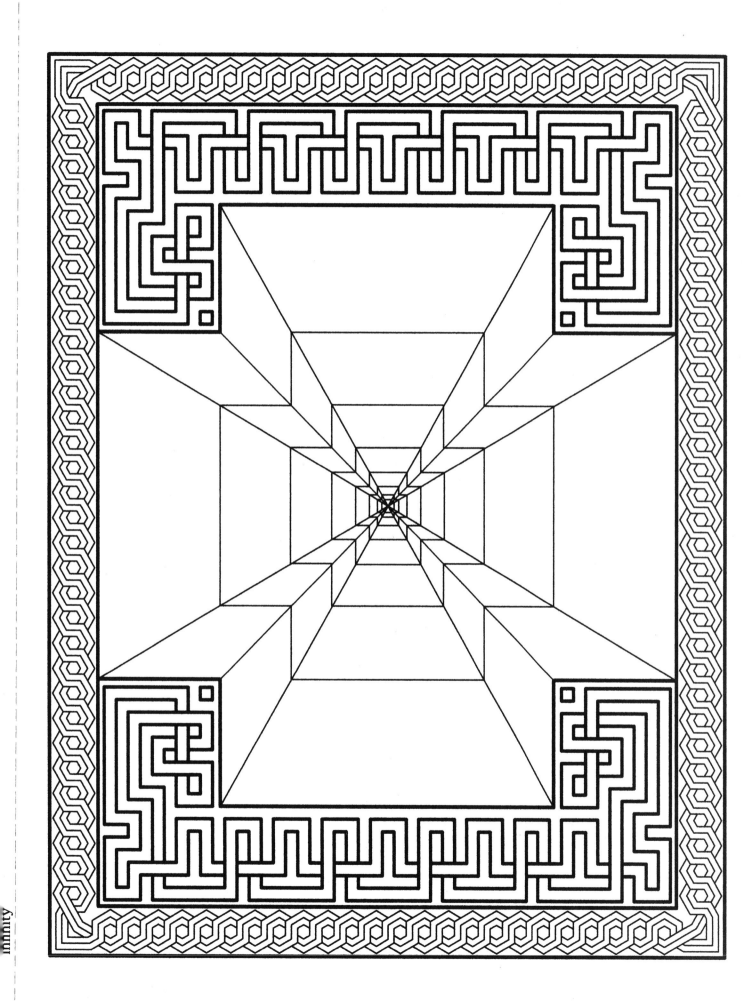

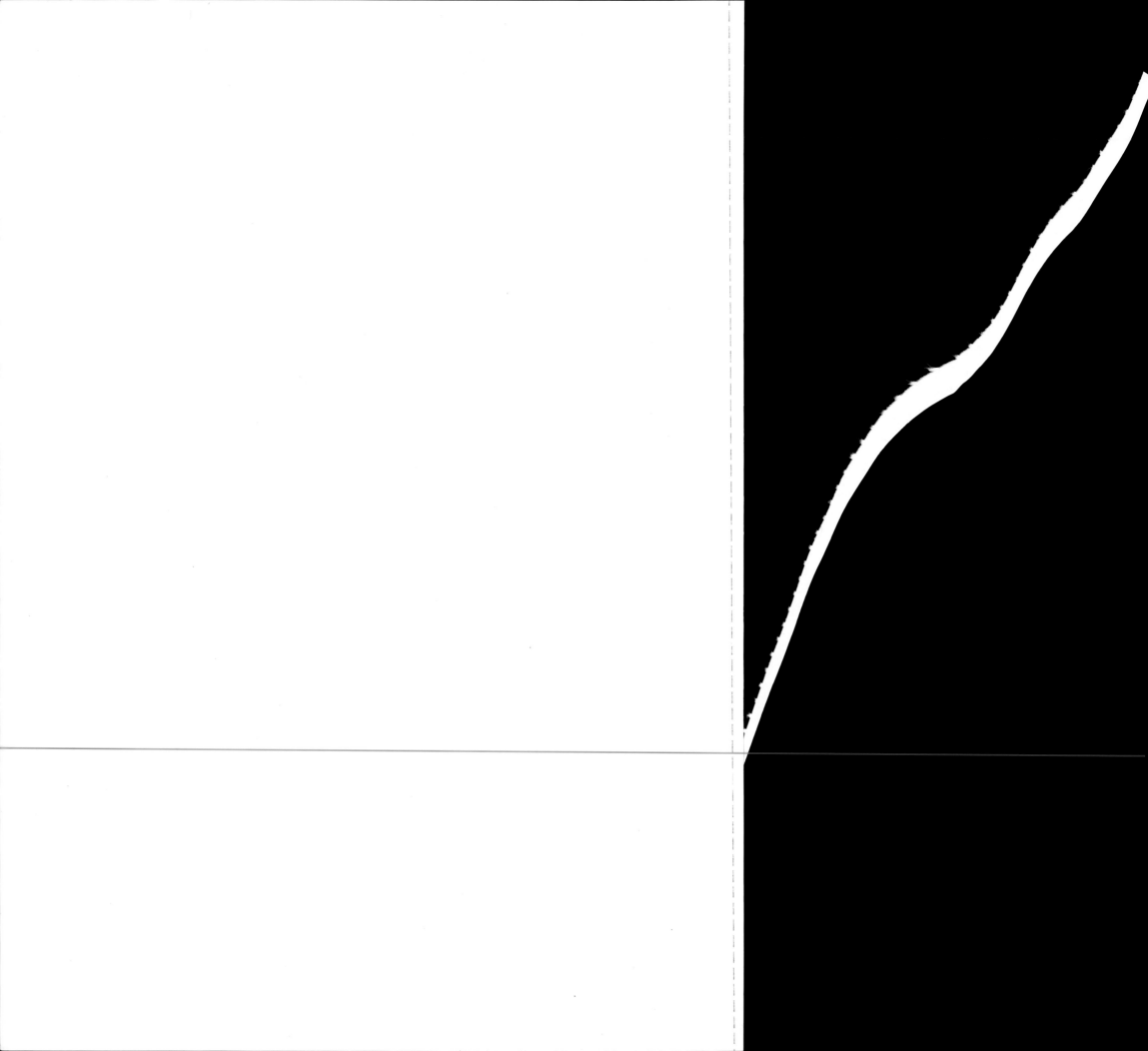

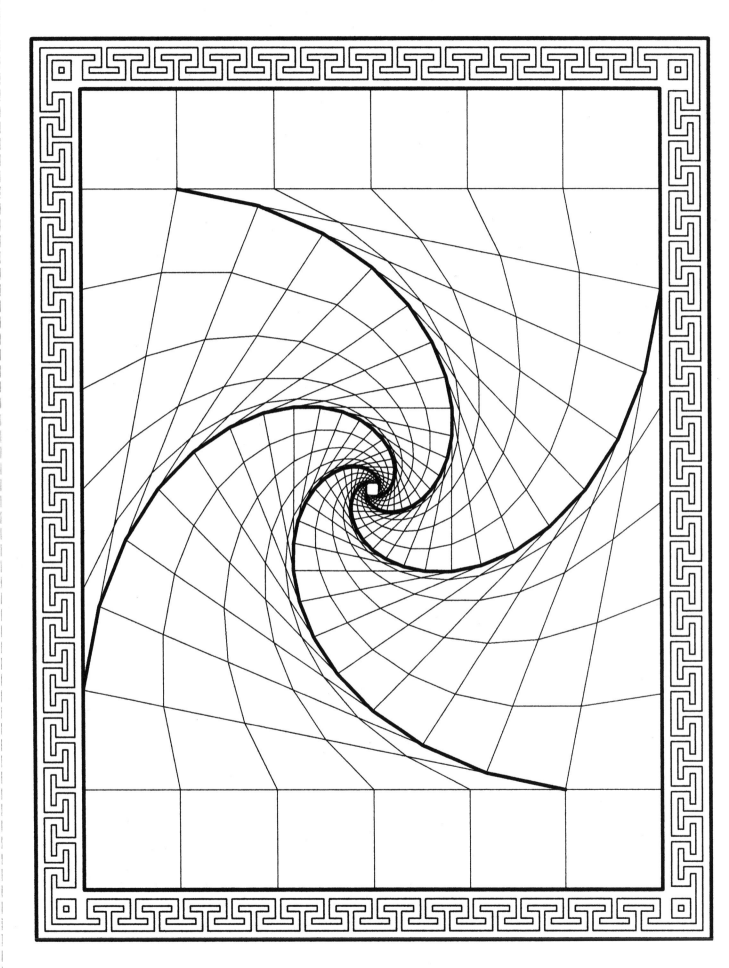

SQUARE
MANDALAS

ALBERTA HUTCHINSON

Mystical Mandala

COLORING BOOK

ALBERTA HUTCHINSON

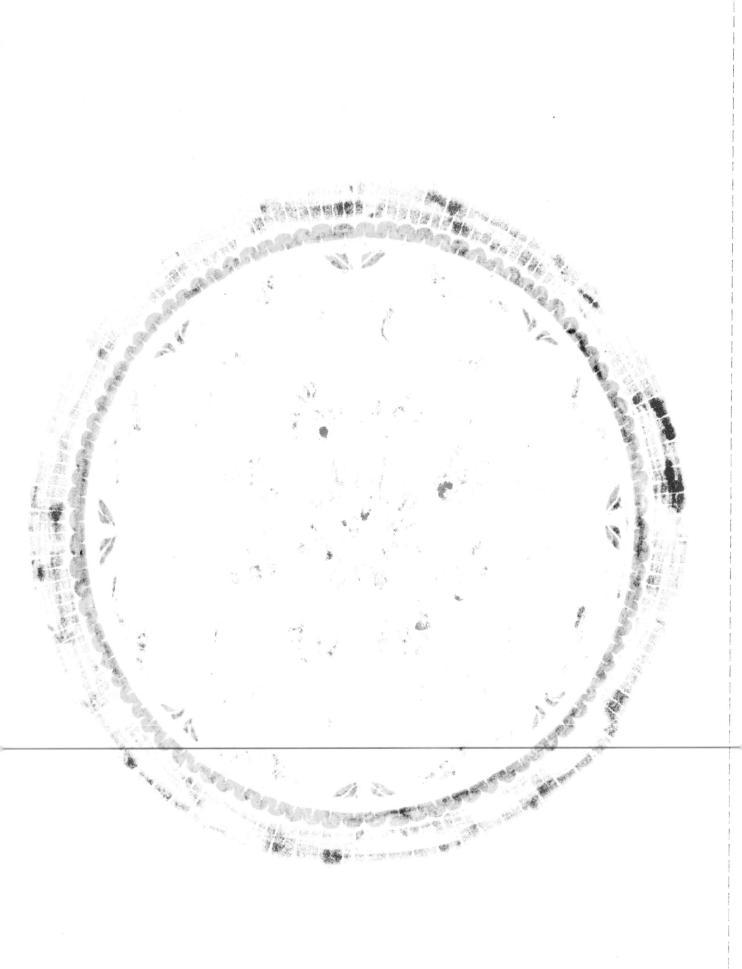